GW00392330

KINGSTON ROAD
REMEMBERED

M.S.B. 1997

WITH THE CRESCENT AND THE CROSS

WEA PUBLICATION

Kingston Road is an important north-south road in Portsmouth part of the main route to and from Fratton. To the north it links up with London Road and to the south Fratton Road. The west side was partly rebuilt in 1934-35 to widen the road which was very narrow.

We have used the 1934/5 Kelly's Directory for our basis, but included some memories from the 1910s to 1920s. Where there was an important building or occupant in the earlier line of buildings we have mentioned that, and we have brought the story up to date as Kelly's directories are no longer published.

Referring to the old prices it may be borne in mind that unemployment at the time was a serious problem and the craftsman was lucky to average £150 per year, whilst the lesser grades earned considerably less. Female employment usually ended upon marriage and earnings were £55 upwards according to situation. National Health deductions were 1/6d (7.5p) weekly and of course , those of income tax, were unheard of among the working classes. VAT did not exist in any form. Dole provided a meagre pittance and recipients were subjected to stringent regulations. Many families remember the Means Test and Boards which had to be attended every few weeks. Nevertheless, many senior citizens will confirm that in those hard times people were more united and helpful towards each other. Crime was considerably less, because offences were far more seriously dealt with.

"Everyone was catered for in Kingston Road – public houses, churches, doctors, cinemas and cafes."

We begin on the west side of Kingston Road, at the junction with Lake Road. The name Kingston may refer to the King's Stone, an ancient boundary mark which legend has it stood in St. Mary's Churchyard to the south. For many years this stone was used by country people who came to the service at the church to mount and dismount from their pillions.

1   Beer Retailer, H Oakshott
    Shown from 1855 to 1875 as Kent's Brewhouse in Lake Road and in 1887 named the Brewery Tap. In 1903 it was altered and by 1903 was known as the Tramway Arms. It was rebuilt when Kingston Road was widened. The old one was in green glazed brick in the Portsmouth United Breweries colours, and stood more in Lake Road than Kingston Road. Since the re-alignment of Lake Road the building stands on the corner of Hanway Road, named

after Jonas Hanway who popularised the umbrella. The pub has since closed and has had several uses.

"They used to have lots of customers – full up every night. It had a bottle and jug, a little Public and a Saloon. If people thought they was too good, they went in there. They were middle class, business people. If they couldn't get in, they'd go to another pub. All ordinary people in working clothes – bricklayers, plasterers, carpenters – went into the Public in their working clothes. Sometimes they used to knock off work and they wouldn't go home 'til closing time. Ladies went in the Bottle & Jug for half a pint of Porter in a jug, or sent the kids up – three or four times. I used to go inside up to a little counter, that came up to waist level when I was a kid. In those days there was no place for kids and you would see them sitting outside on the step drinking a glass of lemonade between seven or eight children, plus an arrowroot biscuit for a penny"

"I used to play the accordion in there sometimes. I couldn't work properly because I wasn't well, and I took up the accordion – and kept my mother after my father died"

Alf Nicholson – Bunky Doodle Ido

Before the road widening the following properties were here:

3   Post Office, John Eccles who was the Postmaster was also a watchmaker. The Post Office closed in 1928.

"Busier than a beehive."

5   Gilbert Pink, Pork Butcher

"Lovely meat"

7   Barratt's Stationers

9   Atkins, Fruiterer

"They has steel inserts in the kerb, into which steel rods of six feet with hooks on the top were put. A tarpaulin went across from the front of the shop and hooked onto the tops of the rods. When it rained it used to fill up with water and we used to poke it to see the water coming through."

11   Riches, Tobacconist also at 214

"A high class shop which sold all the scented cigarettes, all kinds you couldn't get anywhere else."

15-17 Nelson & Co, Domestic Machinery Depot

"The pram and wringer shop"

After widening 3 to 17 were rebuilt as Kingsway Buildings with flats above.

13   Milward & Sons Ltd., Boot & Shoe Retailers

15   Herbert Bell, Fishmonger

17   Rapid Repair Shoe Company on the corner with Sultan Road

When the LDB was bombed in the Second World War they came here in a series of shops occupying 3-11 until the Commercial Road premises were rebuilt.

From 1874 to 1934 Buckland Methodist Church stood on the corner with Sultan Road. The Buckland Methodist Society was started in 1858 in a room over a shop in Fratton Road by members of the Wesley Arundel Street Society. At that time much of the land north of Lake Road, apart from the buildings along Kingston Road, was fields stretching to the foot of Portsdown Hill. By 1870 the land had been earmarked for building purposes and with the increase in population expected the spiritual provision already made was considered inadequate. The Buckland Wesleyan Chapel was opened by the Rev Morley Punshon on 7 May 1875 with seating for 800 to meet this need.

"One door of the church was on the side, and the kerb was less than three feet wide. There was a standard for the tramlines which was about two foot at the base so you could just get by. You had to be careful as the tram came about six inches from the kerb!"

When the corporation decided to widen Kingston Road in 1930 the church authorities asked them to take down the front and build it further back as was done for St Stephen's Mission Hall further north. This was turned down, and the school building in Beeston Street was adapted by the architect Mr Lawrence of Bournemouth in 1936. In 1971 this too was pulled down as part of the Buckland redevelopment.

31   Grays Ltd., Motor Cycle Agents

"There were far more motor bikes about before and just after the war. A lot of people had a bike and a sidecar. They would ride to work all week and then at the weekend, put on the sidecar and go off over the hill with the wife and kiddies. There were Ariels, Matchless, BSA, AJS, Douglas and Royal Enfield, Triumph, Vincent, Rudge, – what great bikes we used to make. All the firms were there, and yet we have been wiped out by foreign bikes."

"A bike would be less than £40. There was a firm in Gosport built bikes – O.E.C. They used to sell them from a place in Stamshaw Road and you can still see the sign up on the side of the building." (This has since gone)

33   Worlds Stores

"Who sold everything as regards delicatessen as well as groceries and provisions. All the nearby grocers were trying to undercut each other – Lipton's, Maypole, Pearks and Home & Colonial all belonged to Associated British Foods, but World's Stores were independent. They sold coconut ice, for 6d a pound, in slices."

Before widening it had been Burchell's Homemade sweet shop.

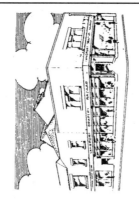

4

"His speciality was egg and butter toffee."

"Burchell's used to make a marzipan stick at Christmas time – like a walking stick of different coloured rock. You had to guess the weight to win it. It was three inches thick and weighed about 10lbs."

35   Knipes, Ladies Hairstylists, still a familiar name in Portsmouth.

"In those days it had cubicles and a wash-basin in each. It was very private – nobody used to see you in your curlers – the curtain was always pulled over. You had permanent waves put in. They also gave you finger waves. They used to press your hair with their fingers and put clips in it 'til it set. People were very hairnet conscious: they'd keep the style for a week and wear a hairnet all day and night. They never combed it out. It cost 12/6d to a pound. They used curling tongs or Marcelle tongs. They did have hair dryers on big stands with elements – big heavy things and dangerous – when you think you used to go in there with steel curlers in your hair! Most ladies only had it done on special occasions, like birthdays and anniversaries. It was an occasion. Other times she'd do it herself with curling tongs'"

Before rebuilding it had been Hoar, the butchers:

"At Christmas time the front of the shop from the roof to the pavement was covered with poultry – and at one side of the shop was a whole bullock. Inside were cages of birds so you could choose a bird and he'd tie a label on it. When the time came he'd kill it for you to take home."

"They had a raffle at Christmas and you put a ticket in all year for a bullock or a whole pig. The bullock was a prize one bought from the show. The winner could claim a prime cut from it for Christmas and the rest went to the voluntary hospitals: the Royal or the Eye and Ear."

Here is Buckland Street

37   George Peters, Wines & Spirits.
        They concentrated mainly on wine. They advertised Admiralty Port
        at 5/- a bottle (25p).

"During Lloyd George's period of office, a non-alcoholic drink was produced and called Lloyd George's Beer. There was a shop on this side of the road with the window painted with dark green paint within two feet of the ceiling. This shop only sold Lloyd George's Beer, and it resembled beer in appearance and sold very cheaply, it proved a very popular line. Even in those days gang warfare was prevalent and there was at least one clash in the shop between a gang from Charlotte Street and another from Stamshaw."

45   Creed & Lawrence, Credit Drapers

"They sold good quality clothing and lots of people bought their clothes on credit. The tallyman came round to collect each week for ladies' gowns, suits, bedding, blankets. Trade fluctuated from week to week otherwise, and the shopkeepers preferred credit because of the regular payments. It was only way people with big families could get things."

47-49 Whittle Bros, Cycle Shop

"They manufactured in a factory in Washington Road, opposite the Shaftesbury. He made two kinds: 'Tantivity, a dearer model with drop handlebars, a light racer with no mudguards for racing and 'Kingston' a cheaper cycle. In 1920's one of his showpieces was a three wheeled dairy cycle with two wheels at the front and one at the back which he made for a dairy at 173 New Road, Moores, in the house set back which you can see from Lynn Road. One of my brothers used to ride at Alexandra Park on a Tantivity. Cycling was very popular in the twenties and thirties. For the Tantivity cycle all accessories from the cycle oil lamp (the best being the King of the Road), down to puncture outfits. Most cyclists carried a repair outfit and on a long country run, a spare inner tube, for the roads were very gritty and a flint could easily cause a flat tyre."

"All bikes were very heavy then: they were upright with roller brakes, or fixed wheel brake, one and a half inch tyres the lot! The Police had specially reinforced frames – they were big burly blokes – and the lamplighters had to have strengthened cross bars to stand on while they turned the gas lights on or off. Ladies' bikes usually had a dress shield on the back wheel – a special mudguard with holes all round and an attachment on the rear hub and the shield laced up with cord between the two. The lights would be carbide – beautifully made brass things with a little red and green light on the sides. You had a silicon carbide block and a water reservoir above. As the water dripped onto the block acetylene gas was given off and that was burned. If you ran out of water on a dark road you can guess what you had to do!"

51   John Long & Sons, Photographer

In earlier times was Stephen Cribb, photographer where everyone went for photos for weddings, football and cricket teams. Stephen Cribb was a noted local photographer whose work is collected now.

"Longs were the only people in the area so everyone went there to get their photos of babies and weddings. I had my wedding photo done there. If it was wet you went to the shop and they laid out a red carpet on the pavement for the bride and all that. If you had your photos done at Longs, you had them done good! I never saw his face because he was always under the big black cloth. He used a big plate camera on a tripod and he did groups and street parties too."

"He was well respected. He took a portrait of my grandfather – with a big table with a pot on it to pose against. All the films were black and white then

but they did tinting by hand to make them coloured – I like the effect myself."
    53   Bollom (Of Bristol), Cleaners and Dyers

"You would have to be a bit better off to use a dry cleaner then but the dyeing – if you had a bereavement you used to take in your best overcoat and have it dyed back. Things were made of natural fibres like cotton and calico and were easier to dye. Poorer people did their own dyeing – if someone had, say, a red dress and it faded she might dye it a darker colour. If a white blouse went a bit greyish or yellow, she might dye it pink or blue. Triplex dyes they were – I remember they made a hell of a mess and were as likely to be a failure as not. Bolloms also used to re-feather your quilts."

    55   Portsmouth & District Foot Hospital – a rather grand name for a chiropodist.

    57   Transport & General Workers Union, Divisional Office.

"57 Kingston Road is the property of the Liverpool Victoria Insurance Society. The rear of the property with an entrance in Arthur Street was leased to the Transport and General Workers Union between 1935 and 1984. Following 1984 to Sogat the printing union. The top floor was accommodation for the caretaker, the rear of the first floor was a meeting hall which was part of the union tenancy, the rest of the first floor was office accommodation for the Liverpool Victoria. The shop fronting the property in Kingston Road had many tenants:– hairdressers, whitewood furniture etc. The union office in 1935 was the base from which most of the pioneering work of the trade union movement was carried out. Mr Sid Webb was the first officer, his secretary Miss Frances Pennicott. These two persons were dedicated to the working class movement. The office was open all day and Bro Webb would hold evening surgeries to resolve problems for members. I as a young trade unionist sat in Sid Webb's office to observe and learn the basic skills needed as a lay officer. On the other side of Arthur Street was Johnson Bros the Chemists and at the far end was a carrier and blacksmith, Mr Cheeseman. Often he would have an audience of children watching him at the forge and fitting horseshoes."

Frank Deacon

    59   Mrs Main, Milliner

"In 1946 the premises housed the PIMCOs Education and Political departments. Now it's a hairdressers. (Since closed)"
here is Little Arthur Street, earlier it was known as Little John Street. The SOGAT Headquarters were built in the street in the 1930s.

    61A   Peter Arnett, Fishmonger

    63   Johnson, Chemist

"He was a bit like Tremletts. He did Annie's Little Liver Pills and Bile

Beans – I used to get those for my granny. You could get lots of herbs – like peppermint and Spanish Liquorice; also Clarke's Blood Mixture at 3/- a bottle. It was to clean your blood and stop you getting boils and spots. It didn't half give you the urge!"

Before widening 63 had been Stroud, the leather merchant:

"He always had a parrot on the windowsill in the nice weather. The trams used to slow down along there, and if you'd missed it you could whistle and they'd let you on. This parrot learned the whistle and many a time the tram would stop when there was no one there."

65-67 David Greig Ltd., Provision Merchants

69-71 William Short, Boot Stores

       Desbois, House Furnishers

       They originally kept a shop in Lake Road selling mostly old furniture and some new. Their store was in North Street. They moved to Kingston Road selling all new furniture, right up until 1981.

"You could get an oak bedroom suite for about 17 guineas.

75 Private House

"With an imitation easel advertising the artist Mr Dowling's trade. He was commissioned to paint the mural on the front when they built the Shaftesbury. It had naked women and so forth. You never saw anything like it in those days and everyone was talking about it. And he fell off the ladder and everyone said it was an Act of God."

83 Sidney Conway, Physician & Surgeon, Medical Officer for Portsmouth Public Assistance.

"In 1910 Dr. Thomas and Dr. Burch were in partnership. Dr. Thomas was by far the more popular, especially with the ladies, for he had the bedside manner. He always had to attend my mother at every birth."

"Dr. O'Connell and his sister later practised there."

"Public Assistance was the forerunner of Social Security, and you had to apply if you were out of work. They imposed the Means Test, and you had to sell even your old piano before they would give you anything. Their records are all in the Central Library. Once in the 1930s their offices in St. Michaels Road were besieged by members of the National Union of the Unemployed and the people inside barred the doors against them."

89 W.H.Fry, Housepainters and Decorators. Before widening they were at number 29.

"It was a yellow painted shop. Some of the shops down Kingston Road were very small, with only a fourteen foot frontage."

91 Edmund Brockway, plumber.

The Brockway family have been connected with Kingston Road for over 150 years. As early as 1832 there was a smithy run by Mr Brockway. In 1887 Samuel Brockway was a Blacksmith and Edward a general smith. Edmund was a plumber from 1899 to 1971! There was plumbing equipment in the window: taps, cisterns etc.

An old cottage style property with peg tile roof, one of the most ancient looking buildings left in the road.

"It was a very small shop with a single gas jet and a board to advertise trade 'Come to Brockways'. He fitted baths but did not sell them – no room."

"Ordinary people didn't have bathrooms then, just an old oval galvanised bath or a bungalow type or a hip bath in the kitchen in front of the fire. Lavatories were outside, usually a lean-to outside the back door but some were still down at the end of the garden. We used to have an old hurricane lamp by the back door and if you went out in a strong wind you were left in the dark. You tried not to have to go and my mother always trained us to go last thing at night. It had a wooden seat which nine times out of ten was riddled with woodworm. The seat had to be scrubbed and where it leaked at the back it would go rotten. Our bowl was white with blue flowers on it – very fancy it was. All the piping was lead then, even fastenings used to hold the pipe on the way were made of lead – a sheet of lead was cut to shape, a hole cut through and then soldered to the pipe. You never had toilet rolls, that was the kiddies' job, tearing newspapers into squares and hanging them on the nail on the wall."

here is Arthur Street

93-95 Portsea Island Mutual Cooperative

Where the Motor Accessories shop is: an older plain nineteenth century house is still visible above.

"It was a small provisions shop originally, but another grocers was built near the Shaftesbury Cinema. It became a hardware shop then. They sold coloured glass which people were putting into their house fronts – it was the fashion. You could get green, red and amber, and a pair cost 3/8d. I did dozens of them. On 10th January 1941 when the main Co-op store in Fratton Road got blitzed it became a general mini Co-op selling anything, because of the lack of buildings. It was shut after the war and then it became a car centre."

"PIMCO divi – in those days they paid a div, it used to be about 1/- or 1/8d, and once they were paying out half a crown. That's a 20% share out. Now they've gone over to those Vista shops in Fratton Road and elsewhere and they don't pay any divi or give stamps. They used to be the poor man's shop but not anymore. The first Co-op in Portsmouth, one of the earliest in the country, was in Charles Street, near St Faith's Church and where it was there now a bench to commemorate it."

97   James Cruikshank, Tailor

"He always had his windows blank. You went in privately, he was a bespoke tailor"

99   Christian Alliance of Women & Girls (Miss R Orchard, sec)

"Old Mr Voller lived in one of a pair of old houses here. He started the corset business opposite."

101-103   Hoopers Ironmongers
        Founded by William Henry Hooper in Broad Street, Old Portsmouth. W.H. Hooper and Hooper & Sons are listed in the directories at Broad Street from 1863 until 1894 variously as Gas Fitter, Optician, Mathematical Instrument Maker, and Ship Instrument Maker. The shop sign board read 'Ship Signal and Lamp Manufacturers, Coppersmiths, and Brassfounders'. By 1896 James Hooper had moved to 57 Kingston Road in premises previously occupied by G. Hemsley, Ironmonger. The company later moved to 101-103 Kingston Road, expanding in the 1960s building across Wellington Place and taking in the former St Stephens Church Hall, which they used as a gardening centre. You can still see the church type roof and rafters inside the shop. The company was last run by the Junipers – Grandsons and great-grandsons of the founder. Since 1983 the shop has been Haskers Carpets and Bedding, the Hooper name continued in much smaller premises nearby for a few years more before closing for good.

107   F. Barnett & Sons Ltd., Fried Fish Shop

109   Mrs L. Anslow, Newsagent

here is Wellington Place

        St Stephens Mission Hall, a mission of St Marys Fratton.

"It was the hall where we used to hold Scout dances and an old boy used to do conjuring tricks. It was the hall for St Stephens Church which stood opposite, next to the Shaftesbury, that was demolished after being bombed in the war. On Sundays there was a Sunday School there."

117   Robert Nelson & Co., Domestic Machinery Depot, formerly at 15-17 Kingston Road.

"I bought my first mangle there."

119   The Shaftesbury Arms, George Whatley

"George Whatley and his wife were here from 1913 until 1957. The old building was demolished in 1931 and business carried on in temporary premises until August 1932 when the new building was opened as The Shaftesbury Arms. The builder was William Hellyer. Before the war bar prices were: Best Bitter 7d a pint, Beer 4d a pint, Light Ale Victory 4d a half pint bottle, Guinness 7d a half pint, Renown Ale 3½d a half pint bottle, lemonade 2d a pint bottle. 2d deposit was charged on bottles taken away and reimbursed on return. On 10th of January 1941 the whole place was ringed by fire but escaped itself. The customers and family left for the safety of an air raid shelter leaving the place empty and open. On return after the All Clear, Mr Whatley found that the firefighters had helped themselves to a drink and the money was all along the counter."

Kathleen Chard

From 1848 to 1902 listed as Buckland Brewery founded by William Allen and run by the family. From 1903 to 1933 it is only listed as a beer retailer until 1934 when it is listed as the Shaftesbury Arms. The brewery at the rear became a Sugar Mill, Burton, Sanders and Son. The building still has a plaque, "Burton, Son and Sanders, Sugar Millers".

The pub had a gloomy sign of Lord Shaftesbury with the Eros statue in the background. He inspired by the Portsmouth cobbler John Pound's example to found the Ragged School movement.

here is Chapel Street

Used to be an ordinary street of terraced houses going down as far as Wellington Place. Wellington Place School was down at one end; one of the few three storey schools built by Portsmouth School Board in 1882, it had big bell tower in the corner It was pulled down in about 1978, when Buckland was being redeveloped. Next there was a piece of waste ground for many decades with hoardings round it – where the petrol station is now.

"On the hoardings you got adverts for things like Portsmouth Park Races where the working man could pay 1/6d to go into the silver ring or in November a match at Fratton Park – First Division would you believe! (Prices in 1934 were a shilling to the ground, 1/6d to the enclosure, south stand 2/6d, and the centre 3/6d) For posh folk the advert offered a dance at the Pavilion Clarence Pier on the Saturday for 3/6d, evening dress, of course."

"There was a Bovril advert on these too that puzzled me as a kid: it showed a bottle of Bovril floating on water and a man sitting astride it in his pyjamas. The caption was 'Prevents That Sinking Feeling'."

On the corner of Washington Road were two little cottages.

here is Washington Road
> 137　The George and Dragon, Reginald Mews
> Listed from 1716 to 1760 as the Cherry Garden. It was renamed in
> 1760 the George And Dragon. It was rebuilt in 1913 to designs of
> local architect A.E. Cogswell. Brown glazed brickwork and half
> timbering above, flying dragons perched on the gables.
>
> 143　Manchester Unity of Oddfellows Hall and Institute, Oddfellows
> Friendly Society (Portsmouth District, Manchester Unity)
> Built in 1926 by Samuel Salter, an imposing white glazed brick
> facade with fluted columns. The badge is a globe topped by a hand
> enclosing a heart.
> Where the offices were, there are now an Indian Restaurant, The
> Ghandi which has been there for sixteen years and a fun pub. The
> main rooms have been converted into the Regal Palace Night Club.
> The Hornpipe Community Arts Centre was there in the eighties.

"The entrance was beautifully paved and there were big mahogany doors
with bevelled glass. You used to go in there with a sort of reverence. I don't
know if it was because we weren't used to something grand. I can remember it
being built. They had a lovely dance floor Below were offices, a lounge and hall
with billiard tables for members. There was a smaller hall upstairs for wedding
receptions if you didn't want the big hall."

"We used to go to dances on Wednesdays and Saturdays. It was 9d to get
in. I don't know why the society was called the Oddfellows. Years before the
National Health Service was started there was a number of friendly societies –
the Oddfellows, the Buffalos and so on. You used to pay about 6d a week
contribution and that entitled you to a doctor, dentist, optician, and so on and it
didn't cost you anymore. They were replaced in the most part by the National
Health Service when it started and now you pay possibly £10 to £12 quid a week
for health insurance. The Buffalos were called the poor mans Freemasons.
Some used to meet at first in the pub to pay your dues – you went down on a
Friday to pay your sixpence – it was an excuse to get out for a booze-up. Our
lodge used to meet in the Lord Clive in Guildford. The Foresters is still in
operation."

> 145　Rd Duke Ladies' Hairdresser

here is Stirling Street, which was built on the site of Swan Farm. The farmhouse
was demolished in 1860. There was a gap from Stirling Street almost to
Dumbarton Street after 1934 where previously there had been numbers 157 to
171.

> 157-163　In 1910 was Sophia Down, pawnbroker.

"Not the kind where people lined up on Monday and got the stuff out at weekends. There were three pawnbrokers in Kingston Road, including N.W. Cousins on the corner of Stirling Street, after Mrs Down, and Bakers on the corner of Toronto Road. People in those days were in dreadful conditions. People on Social Security are a hundred percent better off. You were broke on Monday and had to go to the pawn shop for a few coppers. The pawn shop took in 5,000 bundles a week. There's only two pawn shops left now (1983); Hewetts in New Road, and he's closing down, and Roberts in Fratton Road. People used to buy new clothes and bedding on the weekly, and it would go straight down to the pawn shop and never come out. They still had to pay for it. I don't suppose they got a tenth of it. When I was a kid I used to have half a dozen customers. They used to hide away if they saw someone from the same street going down to the pawn shop. No one wanted them to know."

165   Charles Crease, Greengrocer. After widening he was at 145.

"He carried out a vegetable round in an elaborate horse and cart while his wife and daughter kept the shop."

167   Hawkins, Music Shop

"He knew nothing about music – he was the foreman at Vollers for years until he retired into the shop with his wife."

"He was there in the 1920s and sold mainly stringed instruments: violins and cellos. One of his sons, Bill Hawkins, was a teacher at Stamshaw School and started an orchestra there: we played the march from Scipio, the War March of the Priests, Raise the Flag High and accompanied hymns. In those days you could get a violin for learning for two bob a week – some used to buy by instalments. From that shop many youngsters learnt instruments. It was something in those days to learn the violin. It was generally the piano."

173   Thomas Lewis, Butcher

175   Francis Ward, Confectioner

here was Dumbarton Street

177   Off Licence, Montague Tryon

"Where they sold beer to take away – all different brewers in pints and quarts with the old black screw-in top. You could go into the bottle and jug and buy your beer loose to take away but most people who wanted to drink at home would buy it in a bottle. They also sold fowls' corn because so many people kept chickens. They didn't stock cigarettes – that was at the newsagents, who were open late. They didn't sell wine and for the kids there would be lemonade and ginger beer – no cans of course and not the variety of drinks you get today."

179   Sidney Dennett, Newsagent

"I remember the paper boys gathering round to collect their papers to deliver."

181   Albert Slape, Fishmonger

"Slapes had a reputation for being very high class and all their fish was beautiful. They had no freezers then but down in Portsea they had an ice store where they made big blocks of ice which they had sent up to the fish shops. What they had left over they used to put on top of the fish to keep it fresh in case it wasn't sold so it would last until the next day. When they put the fish out they put all ice in between on the marble slab. The counter was always marble and on the slope so that the melted ice could drain at the bottom. They sold mackerel, cod, bloaters and kippers. Slapes in Lake Road used to smoke their own fish. They had crabs, lobsters, oysters, cockles, sprats, trout and so on. You used to go and ask for a bit of salt fish. They would weigh up what you wanted. Most often a working man would have a different bit of fish every night – it was cheaper than meat and they used to believe in the old days that fish made your brains. There were all sorts of stories to make children especially eat their food – crusts to make your hair curl, carrots help you see in the dark and so on. Arnetts, at number 58, were much cheaper. They has several shops. Slapes charged a bit extra but they had their customers who came in from all over Portsmouth because they knew it was just that bit better. The fish came in by rail sent down from Grimsby mainly. It came in cases all in ice and early in the morning the shop keeper would go down and get his fish for that day. The fish market was where it is now more or less, just a bit further up this way now, and it has been built all brand new in Durham Street, near the station about three years ago."

183   Ebb Stapleford, Undertaker. They also had a shop in Arundel Street.

"People wore mourning then although it started to go out after the First World War. The men wore black tie and perhaps an armband and maybe a widow would wear a black veil. Widows often wore black for three to six months after a death and a few wore it all their lives. Us kids used to wear a black diamond on our sleeve. Everyone in the street used to close their curtains and on the actual day of the funeral, walk to the main road. I think you see not so many funerals now – then people used to die young – the kids used to die of scarlet fever and diphtheria and it was common to see funerals."

185   Alfred Cook, Hairdresser

187   F. Barnett & Sons, Fried Fish. They also had a shop at 107.

189   Albert Green, Hairdresser

191   The Bedford Arms, Sidney Etherington

        Listed from 1874 to 1887 as the Bedford Arms and then from 1888 to 1974 as a beer retailer. It was a Langford's brewery house.

"It was a funny old pub – homely and old fashioned."

here was Bedford Street
193   Price Bros, Bakeries
"A big place, specialising in 'wedding slices' made on a big tray with all the silver balls, cut into slices just like you might have a slice of wedding cake. It cost the princely sum of 2d each."
195   George Martin, Medical Herbalist – a firm still going strong in Kingston Crescent.
197   Princes, Boot Maker
"He used to stand near the window and repair the shoes – 2/9d for ladies and 3/3d for gents, for sole and heel and an extra 3d or 4d if they were tipped with rubber – and for boys 6d if they were tipped with steel in the toe and heel. Although that seems cheap by today's reckoning it was surprising the number of shoes and boots that were left there. When the business closed down a lot were thrown away. They had never been claimed. He'd spent his time soling and heeling them and it was all wasted because people couldn't afford to collect them."
207   Alfred Edney, Garage
"Edney was taxi driver. If you wanted one of his taxis you had to go in the Whitehall to find him. He only died about seven years ago (1983)"
"It brings back a few old memories of the Morris 8 which could be bought in those days for £118. The tax was £6."
209   Chapman's Laundry, Receiving Office
"It was a front room converted. The lady used to stand there and do the collecting: sheets and shirts on Mondays and Tuesdays and on Fridays and Saturdays was their busiest time because people used to come and get their husband's stiffened collars for Sunday wear. Most of the men who went out in their Sunday best wore a stiffened collar, and Chapmans used to do it very nicely. They charged 7d. Their laundry was at the end of Kingston Crescent, run by Annie Oliver, a formidable town councillor who imposed a harsh discipline on her girls."
211   William Laversuch, Clothier
215   The Whitehall, Robert Cleall
        Known as the White Swan until 1920 which had a skittle alley behind.
"Its been brightened up over the years."

here is Malthouse Road, named after the Malthouse for Kingston Brewery, on the site in 1870, had fine brick and tile houses with imposing doorways on the south side, perhaps connected with the brewery in earlier days. They were demolished in the early 1970s.

217-221   Was the Kingston Brewery from 1785 to 1964 under various owners – John Norris (1785-1788), William Fidlin (1789-1830), Richard Murrell (1835-1879) his initials appear above the shop U-Name-It, Geo Peters (1885-1910), Ernest Whicher (1911-1915), Hammerton & Co Bottling Plant (1917-1948), Charrington & Co Bottling Store (1953-1964). Part of the site became the Majestic Cinema.

219-221   Hammerton & Co., brewers of malt stout.

"They had an off licence in the road and the actual brewery was in Malthouse Road. In its later years, it was really a bottling plant: it was mostly girl labour dressed up with coarse sack aprons and perhaps a bit of waterproof round it and great big clogs on and a handkerchief round their head. They looked like they worked in the mills. They did work hard, they washed all the bottles. The bottles were filled automatically but washed by hand. The bottles had screw tops made of a forerunner of plastic, never any colour but black. The bottles were threaded inside and an advertising label was stuck over the top and down the side to seal it. They used to make a lovely stout – Hammerton's Malt Stout – my favourite that was, the best medicine you could take – better than Clarke's Blood Mixture."

The Majestic

"It was built in 1921 by a Portsmouth builder, Richard Stokes, at a cost of £50,000. £20,000 more than the Odeon, North End, fifteen years later. It was just as grand as a theatre.

"A man named Fyfield did the brickwork there and my brother was an apprentice to him and helped him build it. The front is artificial stone and granite with a pediment and fluted Doric columns, three cathedral windows and an overhanging portico. The front entrance is very grand with two mahogany pay boxes, marble stairs and marble and mosaic panelling. Ventilation was by air drawn from outside, heated and forced around concealed ducts by electric fans. The interior plaster work was beautiful: done by a Milanese artist called Carlo. The ceiling with oversize light fittings, three torch chandeliers, remains but I remember seeing the plaster work dolphin from the curving balcony in pieces in the yard when it was converted into a snooker club.

"There were four side boxes, just like a theatre, and tropical scenery was painted in cove panels, lit by hidden lights. The original colour scheme was

The Majestic

brown and Tripoli grey with a pink border and a roof of glistening gold.

"Us kids used to go in the afternoon and pay 3d. Most picture houses were 3d. There were lovely blue plush seats that we'd never heard of before. In the days of silent films there was a lady on the piano or maybe a man singing and for war films there was a man with a cap pistol. If there were songs in the big films (or epics as they used to call them) a man would come from the local choir and sing the songs in a little pit. The Majestic was the first to have an orchestra. The leader was Mr. Peters. When they were dancing in the film the orchestra would play some lovely pieces by Franz Lehar and it was really grand. They had a commissionaire which we'd never seen before. I can see him now in his blue uniform with epaulettes and gold tassels and beautiful buttons, a half Sam Brown belt round his waist and his trousers with a stripe – like a major-general from some Imperial Army he stood in the steps. He used to give a continuous spiel about the film and the prices. Seats upstairs were 1/6d, downstairs were about 6d and 9d for the evening performance. In the old days you always had the performance two and a half hours with about an hour in between. They started continuous performances so you could go in anytime. They had a chucker-out especially for the kids. It was one of the few cinemas in the town you might go to twice a week because they changed the programme on a Wednesday and a Sunday. It was always full – no matter when you went there it was always full.

"My mother went there as a cleaner and she was still working there when she was about 70 years old. All the ice cream papers and so on used to disappear off the floor overnight and when the painters came in they found hundreds and hundreds of papers up behind the screen where the rats had taken them up.

"In later years the big cinema chains had begun to monopolise the film industry. Because they could offer multiple outlets to the distributors they were in an ideal position to bid for the best film of the day as soon as they were released, and the independents were gradually pushed into the back seat. The big companies began building the Odeons and others seating 1,500 or more in the thirties and after that the smaller halls gave up the unequal fight. In 1950 the Majestic was faced with new safety demands which would have meant buying the neighbouring buildings to provide fire exits and it was then sold to Essoldo. It was later known as the Classic, but in 1973 the cinema closed. The council wanted to pull it down and build houses on the site, but various people including the projectionist of the Rex, the City Architect and the Portsmouth Society wanted to save it as the most opulent cinema in the city. After drastic alterations it reopened in 1976 as a billiard and snooker club."

227-229   R.G.Hoile & Co. Ltd., Cabinet Makers

Smith & Vosper, Pastry Cooks was on the corner with Kingston Crescent until 1928 when the road was widened and they rebuilt the White Hart on the new corner. The White Hart later became the Hampshire Building Society, which was taken over by Bradford & Bingley, currently the building is empty.

"Smith & Vosper's cakes were out of reach. The most exclusive thing they had was their sponge cakes. Kept in a glass case on the counter, they went up to 4d each. To get one you had to have double pneumonia or scarlet fever otherwise you were pushed past the door with your tongue hanging out."

"The old way into the pub round the corner where they done the horses in the days of stage coaches was there. The pavement in Kingston Road was only 2' 6" wide, so if you went out into the road to pass a lady with a pram you were just as likely to get run over by a tram."

This junction, where London Road, takes over from Kingston Road, is known as Kingston Cross, an old name mentioned in the grant of the borough to the corporation of Portsmouth by Henry III. In a map of 1823 it is shown as 'Stone Cross', now called Kingston Cross. Some local tradition talks of a Saxon cross and a gibbet.

We now turn into **Kingston Crescent**: a curving road connecting with the top of Commercial Road, where many of the magnates of nineteenth century Portsmouth had fine houses.

South Side

118   Beer Retailer, Mrs Rosina Collins

The Sportsman. Listed from 1887 to 1934. It was a Jewell's brewery house, previously known as the Eagle in 1867. It was demolished when Kingston Road was widened.

116   White Hart, Charles Le Metty

A Pike Spicer house listed from 1823 until 1964. It was demolished when Kingston Road was widened and rebuilt.

114   Reginald Lodder, Hairdresser

112   Edward Evans, Fruiterer

106-104   Harvey & Son, Decorators

Was earlier S.A & W. Lillington, established 1810, practical plumbers and decorators, electric light and bell installations, gas and hot water fitters, Kingston Cross, Landport quotes an advert in St Marks Church magazine of 1898.

100   Albert Flowers, Market Gardener and potato merchant whose

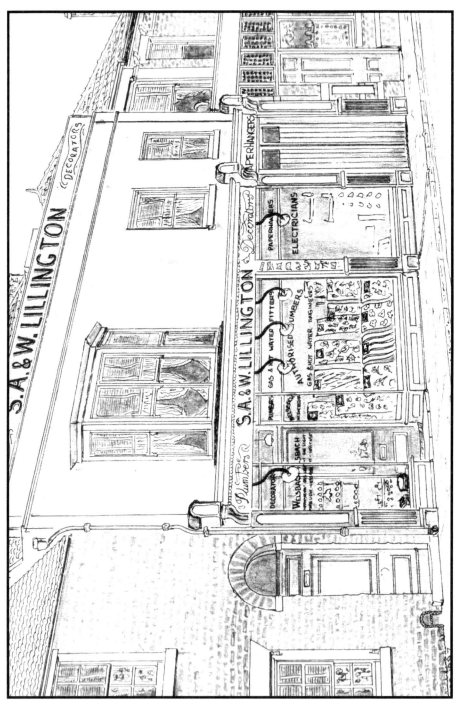

Lillingtons

residency seems to have started the story of it being a farmhouse. Kingston House, a huge blue brick Georgian mansion in its own grounds with fine plaster ceilings and an imposing pillared doorcase (now in St Thomas Street, Old Portsmouth). It was occupied by Richard Murrell of the Kingston Brewery, and later a lady blue stocking whose father was a councillor, so some meetings were held in the fine rooms. It was pulled down as a dangerous structure in the early 1970s despite being a listed building. Archaeologists found evidence of Saxon occupation on the site, and a massive ugly factory building now occupies the site. This has been empty for some years and there are proposals to build housing on the site.

"It was a very large and grand but unoccupied. It was cared for by a neighbour who would occasionally change a piece of gingham material of various colours to show that the house was still occupied, or owned by somebody."

Una Jarman

94   William Hale, Outfitter
92   Ernest Watts, Credit Draper
90   The Admirals Head, James Garnett.
      A Pikes brewery house. Listed from 1823 to 1981. In 1983 it was converted into offices.

here is Gamble Road
86   Edward Butler, Decorator
      Called Toronto House
84   Portsmouth Hostel for Boys (C. Milford, sec.)
82   Royal Naval Lodge of Oddfellows (Manchester Unity) (Edwin Heather, Secretary)
      Liverpool Victoria Insurance Offices (D Roberts)
      "Before National Health you used to take your card in for insurance – a penny policy Life Insurance. It was your burial money really, enough to cover a funeral. Men used to come around for your premiums and they used to give you your new insurance card year by year. If you were not insured it was doubtful whether you got yourself protected, before National Health. Or your employer – it was quite a rigmarole. When your card was full you took it to the society you belonged to. Others were the Foresters, National Fireman's Society, Britannic Assurance Company, the Manchester..."
      Royal Naval & Marines Commissioned & Warrant Officers Death Benefit Association (Lieut.-Comdr. Herbert Rose, Sec)

80   Rev Hy. Gooch, Vicar of St Stephens

76   James Davis M.B., ch.B., B.A.O., L.M., Physician, Medical officer Landport district, City of Portsmouth Public Assistance Committee & medical officer to H.M. Prison.
Listed from 1962 to 1964 as St Theresas Grammar School, Ladies of Mary.

"Doctors Davies, Sawyer and Treharne held surgery in one of the large houses in Kingston Crescent. Dr Davies being the senior partner, lived in the flat above the surgery. He had a black Riley car with red spoked wheels which everybody in the area recognised.

If a home visit was needed it cost 2/6d, or a half a crown. One day my younger sister needed a home visit for an abscess on her knee, so my mother paid the half-crown. My sister had seen the car coming up the road and, deciding the visit was not for her, hobbled up the road and burst the abscess herself!

The surgery itself had a substantial waiting room but most of the space was taken up by a large Morrison table air-raid shelter. There were a number of chairs around the room for the patients waiting to see the doctor."

Una Jarman

74-72 Rev Henry Parnaby, Congregational
Later Daley's Private School, Misses L.K. & M.R. Daley. Listed from 1938 to 1958

"The uniform worn by the girls attending the school included a striped blazer of green and navy blue. The stripes were about 1½ inches wide. The girls did not live locally but came from further afield where money was more available for an education and a blazer of that type"

Una Jarman

70   Portsmouth North Conservative & Unionist Association (Admiral of the Fleet Sir Roger Keyes, Bart, G.C.B., K.C.V.O., C.M.G., D.S.O., LL.D., D.C.L., M.P., President)

66   St Theresas Grammar School, Ladies of Mary. Listed from 1962 to 1964

64   Douglas Bevis, Dental Surgeon

62   Was in 1948 a temporary Unitarian Christian Church

60   Joseph McCalden B.A.,M.B.,B.ch., Physician & Surgeon

52   Rev Francis Cleverdon, Curate of St Stephens

48-42 A & E Chapman, Laundry

"Chapmans laundry was situated in Kingston Crescent, Portsmouth, covering about five acres between the Crescent and Garfield Road. Mrs Annie Oliver inherited the original hand-wash laundry from her mother Mrs Chapman, and she then proceeded to enlarge and improve it, incorporating a large transport section, and employing several hundred people. She was later awarded the O.B.E. for her services during the war, and became a Portsmouth City councillor.

The girls at Chapmans worked long hours in unhealthy conditions with fluff from the materials always in the hot atmosphere. TB was not uncommon, and many girls died from the effects.

At the outbreak of war men were called up, and girls were attracted to the Womens' Land Army and the Wrens, so many of the heavier jobs had to be managed by older women.

The Company was very much a family affair, and my brother and I - now in our seventies - both worked for Chapmans. Wallie (my brother) became an engineering apprentice, and I worked for nine years in various departments, and in my leisure time played in the band for the staff dances. In one department I learned to repair nylon stockings which were very scarce in those days. The ladders had to be machined together with a fine hook, it was very tedious work.

The apprentices served a five year training term on very poor wages. The engineering department had to maintain and repair all the mechanical machinery - the washing machines, the enormous ironing cylinders called "big eights", shirt machines, goffering irons, and of course the large boilers which provided steam and hot water. All this machinery and equipment was getting older as the war progressed. On one occasion the stock of boiler fuel coal caught fire and took several months before finally being put out.

I also remember the apprentice's pranks - kippers being stuffed behind hot pipes - but they didn't want to get caught, as an interview with Mrs Oliver was a terrifying event. The boys also had the horrendous job of descaling the cooled boilers during the works holidays. This required getting inside the boilers and scraping the chalk from the sides.

Many a dance was held in the canteen, of course the Navy would accompany the girls and subsequently many married sailors. The sad thing I vividly remember was the whole laundry staff being assembled in the canteen by Mrs Oliver to be told that a ship had been torpedoed with the resulting tragic loss of life. Many girls had married and become widows in a very short time.

I also remember those weddings. Having worked in the canteen, on one occasion I helped get the wedding breakfast for my friend who married a sailor, changed into a (borrowed) bridesmaid's dress, returned from the Church to help serve the food, then joined the band to dance the night away. On the way home I was stopped by a policeman because my bicycle lights were faltering. I was carrying my accordion at the time and had to cycle back to Cosham."

Joan Palmer (Nee Errington)

40   Was from 1867 to 1898 the Travellers Joy a Miles brewery house.
6   Solomon Criger, Dentist

At Commercial Road we cross over and return on the north side

1D   Frank Marsh, Tobacconist
1B   Chapman's Laundry, Receiving Office
5   Charles Warren, Boot Repairer
9   Crescent Arms, a Lush's Brewery house. Listed from 1886 to 1964.

here is Mills Road, earlier known as Mushroom Street

11   Miss Emily Trayte, Second Hand Bookseller
13   Miss S. Trayte, Dolls Hospital
15   Royal Dragoon, listed from 1904 to 1970. It was earlier known as the Crescent Brewery Tap from 1886 to 1902.
17   Smeed & Smeed Ltd., Wine & Spirit Merchants
17A Mrs Millicent Anthony, Servants' Registry Office
25   William Stone L.D.R.C.S.Eng Dental Surgeon
25A Rev Rd. Parsons, Curate of All Saints
27   Lillie & Co, Baltic Timber Yard from 1934 to 1940. Earlier A.E. Porter J.P. lived here.
37   Miss Louisa Warden, Dress Maker
39   Daley's Commercial School, Miss M. Daley from 1923 to 1934.
41   Miss Patience Baker L.L.A.M., Teacher of Dancing. Was earlier the home of Frank Bevis, Oatlands
     Trafalgar Sports Club (H. Millett, President)
     Portsmouth & District Cyclists' Touring Club
     Portsmouth North End Cycling Club
     Winters' Sports & Social Club (J. Walmsley Sec)
43   Was earlier the home of the Seagrove family
     47-49 Lynton House School, Miss Thorpe & Miss Hemsted, listed from 1923 to 1940.
65   George Price, Dentist
79-81 Andrews & Son, Undertakers. Although the business was by now run by Stephen Brading.
83   George Cooper, Wine Merchant

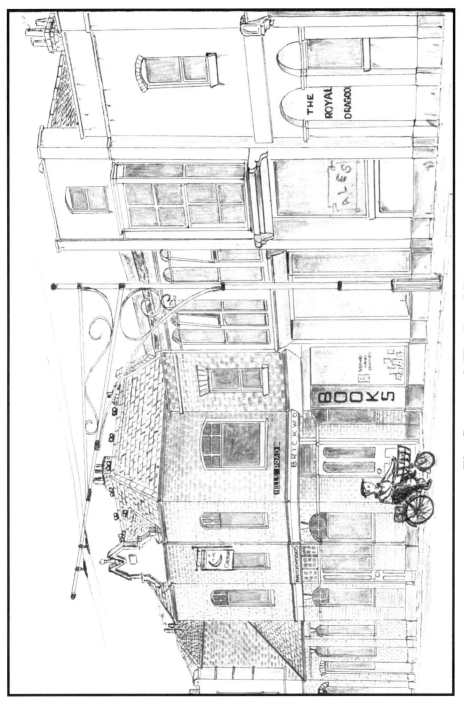

The Crescent & The Royal Dragoon

85-87 Cranstone & Sons, Drapers
   Started by Midhurst born James Cranstone who came to Portsmouth
   in 1865 and is listed as a Linen draper at Kingston Cross.

here is Pitcroft Lane
   89-91 Montague Burton Ltd., Tailors

"Kingston Crescent has another claim to fame: in 1932 a famous amateur film maker featured in Bioscope Days had a studio there, a large wooden hut like a village hall complete with a stage used as a set filled with cameras and lighting gear. He used the beaches at Eastney and Hayling Island for location work. He was interested in special effects and developments in sound. He held a fireworks party, inviting dozens of children including myself."

   To the east of Kingston Cross was Kingston Farm, farmed by the Playfoot family for 200 years and sold for building land in 1872.

East Side
   "Tramcars plied in both directions to Cosham way and linking up with Fratton Road in the other direction. Except for below the waist these drivers were fully exposed to all weather conditions and so dressed accordingly – the leather soles on their boots would be ¾ of an inch thick, heavy coats and always long woollen gloves. These cars could not be reversed but, as the driving mechanism was exactly the same at each end, all it meant was to remove two brass handles, one for contact and one for brake, and put them on the other motor. Warning other traffic was done by a bell, operated by the foot. At the centre of the top deck would be a strongly sprung connecting arms, to the overhead wire with an eye attached to the further end. To transfer this to the overhead line for the opposite journey the conductor had a long pole with a hook at the end which was always stowed at the side of the tram. As this was operated at ground level, a new conductor would have difficulty in making the connection with flashes flying everywhere. There were sections and not as today you only paid for the distance travelled."

   Kingston Cross is a short stretch of road from London Road to Kingston Road.
   Opposite Kingston Crescent was a Police Station
   "On the upper floor there were about 320 policemen and above 15 were attached permanently to the Fire Service. When I first joined the fire brigade they came under the police."

George Smith

North End Library

"This was not furnished as one gets today, for the weekly and daily newspapers were attached to high stands and some read them standing up. Periodicals and magazines were digested sitting on hard wooden chairs and the scope of the lending books could in no way be compared with today."

National Provincial Bank

Taylor & Sons Dairies (1912) Ltd.

Isaac Michaels, Costumier

Blue Anchor Hotel, Ernest Bell

A fine three storey pub bombed in the war and rebuilt in curious bungalow style marks the beginning of London Road on the east side.

Kingston Road east side

252   George Peters & Co.Ltd., Wine Merchants

250   Harry Hankers, Butcher

248   George Kent, Boot Manufacturer

246   James Baker, Wool Merchant

244-242   J.J. Joyce Ltd., Drapers

240   PIMCO Butchers

"The butchery department was in Basin Street in what was originally a tram shed with horse stables. You can still see the stone Co-op Butchery 1937. The butchery was transferred to the old cinema, the Eagledrome, in New Road. After the war they had a place for Co-op workers and street cleaners. They'd never had such a nice place to go. Before then they only had a dirty wooden hut in the yard. Now the Co-op Workers Club has a place further down Kingston Road."

here is Basin Street

"This name has always puzzled me: there's no canal or inlet anywhere near. During the First World War and years after there was a slaughter house at the far end, so it was a common sight to see cattle driven to their doom. There was a passageway known as Jonathan Alley through to Powerscourt Road, (Later Basin Path, now widened into a road and part of Basin Street). Up to the war the Farlington Laundry was there, it was taken over by Airspeed during the war. In the second world war the depot in Basin Street became an ARP station. The rescue people were killed when the bomb fell in Powerscourt Road. Also on the south side was a brewer from at least 1870: it was John Wright, botanical brewer in 1910, later Strawson's Mineral Waters, later still SOTA."

238 N.S. Harvey & Co.Ltd., Tobacconists, he also has a shop in Albert Road.

"We used to smoke a lot in those days. IN 1931, he was the first to have a licence. He used the initials R.V on his packages. When the baccy was sold it had red wrappers with R.V on them. He also sold loose tobacco at 8d an ounce – now it's £3.48 for Gold Shag. Some tobacco was grown in Hampshire near Odiham and marketed in Salisbury. It burnt very quickly and was very black. Navy twist was like as rope, very dark, and people cut it up. In those days ten Woodbines were 4d but don't forget wages are higher now."

236   Stanley Coxon, Newsagent

"Outside the newsagents a placard of the Evening News tells us Councillor Frank J Privett J.P. has been chosen as our Lord Mayor for Jubilee year (1935). The next placard gave a sad item of news "Docky dies on way home." Closer inspection of the paper informs us that he collapsed on a bus travelling in Edinburgh Road. My favourite newspaper was the Daily Mirror, not so much for the news, but at my young age I did enjoy following the adventures of Pip, Squeak and Wilfred in the strip cartoon. Pip was a black dog, Squeak was a penguin, and Wilfred a rabbit with big floppy ears. They were the goodies in the story and a villain was a weird looking person called Bolshevik, with his dog, Popski. During the firework period the shop would have these on sale, Standard was a popular brand. I believe we made better guys in those days than they do today. We would stuff a sack with old paper, rags, straw or even leaves, tie the bottom to form the head, drape an old coat and trousers over the sack, stuffing the arms of the coat and the legs of the trousers. A cardboard mask for a face, some whiskers stuck on, could be bought for a penny. A cloth cap surmounted the final effort. This was propped up in the old box or cart or possibly in a borrowed pram with a cocoa tin for a collection box. Fireworks were named Little Demons, Flitter Fountains, Jumbo sparklers, all at a halfpenny. A good fountain was 2d and a Parachute Floating Light cost a shilling. Also in the Evening News were adverts for coal at 46/- (£2.30) a ton and this was best Yorkshire nuts, from Fraser & Whites. The Co-op charged a shilling less for their best nuts. Another advert offered a Philips six valve superheterodyne wireless for less than twelve guineas. Or you could have an Ecko wireless receiver for ten and a half guineas – in easy terms 3/6d a week."

Frank Ford

234   Freeman, Hardy & Willis, Bootmakers.

"Charles Clore had three different companies Freeman, Hardy & Willis, Frisby and Trueform for the same reason as Princes Stores,"

232   Prince's Stores, Provision Merchants

"They did cut price. He also ran another shop near the model railway shop in Fratton Road in a different name. At one period he swapped the name over because one shop was going down in trade. They used to do that quite a lot. Eventually the Kingston Road shop closed. If you notice, the tops of the shops are all different because they were blown off when one of the first bombs of the Second World War dropped on the Blue Anchor. There is a date stone up there."

> For the past 34 years has been Solent Sewing Machine Co. They repair and sell sewing machines of all types, from home to large industrial.

224-222   Thomas Collins, Draper

220   E.W. Honess & Sons, Dyers & Cleaners

218   Maynards Ltd., Confectioners

> There until fairly recently. (1983)

216   J. Baker & Co.Ltd., Outfitters. They has branches throughout the city.

> The firm was founded by John Baker, first chairman of Portsmouth School Board, the first board in Hampshire after the 1870 Education Act. The Portsmouth Board built New Road School, Cottage Grove, Drayton Road, Wellington Place and George Street schools: altogether 24 schools up to 1902. John Baker was twice Liberal M.P. for Portsmouth and was knighted.

"A better class of outfitter: we didn't buy anything there."

"They used to sell all the school uniforms, caps and blazers, trousers, blouses and skirts, all in the school colours. They did the embroidered badges as well."

214   Herbert Riches, Tobacconist

"A high class tobacconist."

"When decimalisation came in, he was violently opposed to it and he wouldn't change his prices. He kept the old penny and shilling prices. He thought he was going to make people keep to the old system. But within a fortnight from 15th February 1971 there was no old money in circulation – except that he had previously got in a stock of old coppers. You had to pay in silver and he'd try to pay your change in old coppers. Eventually he fell foul of the Decimal Act and had to give it up."

"Like all such shops they had a hairdressers at the back."

212   Madame Florence, Ladies Fancy Drapery

> The shop was run by Miss Florence Terry at one time.

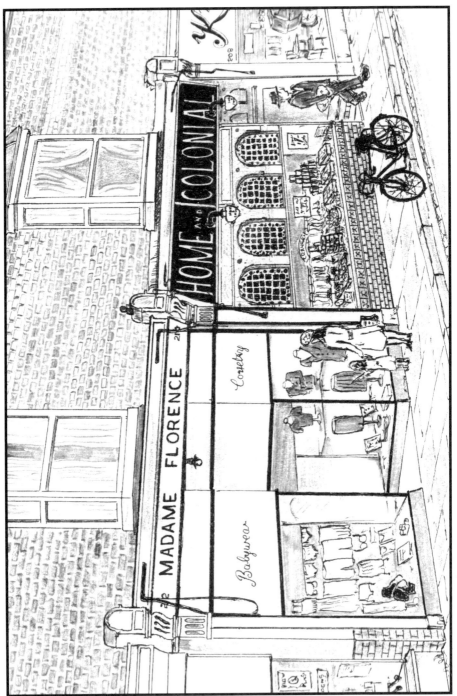

Madame Florence

"About 1948 I sometimes accompanied my mother to the shop. It was run by two middle aged ladies. The shop sold other things but mostly ladies' underwear. In this day and age no one has seen anything like it. My mother would purchase her corset/stays colour pink with laces, hooks, eyes and bones, which when she arrived home was adjusted to her size. I thought it was a contraption of torture. They also sold knickers so large one could get your whole body in them. The colour of peach seemed very popular. Also for winter wear one could buy the same garment fleecy lined. When the goods were paid for in stirling the bill could be £2 2s 2¾d, any change amounting to a farthing, which was a small coin with a robin on it, would be given to you in a packet of gold pins instead of the coin. I think this was one of the last shops in Portsmouth dealing in farthings."

Una Jarman

216-212   Is now the Far Eastern Stores run by Mr David Lai who came here in 1975. With Mrs Lai and two Mr Lees, the business sells mostly food but utensils and ornaments are available. Mr Lai is also involved with the Chinese Community Association based at 208.

210   Home & Colonial Stores Ltd.
With fancy moulded glass windows, one of the nicest shop fronts in Kingston Road. Now Bowers, the leather shop.

208   William Keast, Baby Carriage Maker.
"They was always bought on tick. A pram would cost 2/- a week"
Behind this row of shops were some tiny cottages, Paradise Row from 1830 to 1867, from 1886 to 1891 Paradise Gardens. The only sign of this old street is the single storey shop that was built over the entrance.

206   David Stubbington, Tailor
later Goldfingers, hairdressers.

204   Joseph Frisby, Boot Shop
"His boots started at 4/- a pair. Up to the Second World War most people repaired their own. Repairs at the shop were 1/9d sole and heel. Boots and shoes were all leather in those days, none of this man made stuff."

200   Arthur Bull Ltd., China, Glass, Hardware & Toys
"He had another big shop on the corner of Norfolk Street and Kings Road selling china, glass and hardware. He sold good stuff."
"There was a very large corner house and the occupant was Mr. Bendell in 1910. With Mr White he had a flourishing haulage business. Mr Bendell was Yeomanry. The Salvation Army held services in the roads as they do now,

and one of their spots was outside his house in Powerscourt Road. On one occasion he hired a window cleaner who lived in Bedford Street who threw open his side window, had a bass drum on a stool inside, and throughout the service the window cleaner punched the drum."

"There were riots against the Salvation Army along the south coast at this time. An effigy of Sarah Robinson was burnt in public."

Rowe, the blacksmith was just inside Powerscourt Road

"He was one of the last blacksmiths in Portsmouth. I remember I went in there to get something made. I used to get our iron hoops repaired. He used to wait until there was a whole pile to do, to weld them."

here is Powerscourt Road

- 198 Poirett, Gowns
- 196 Arthur Goddard, Chemist
- 194 Thomas Durant, Butcher
- 190 George Mason, Picture Frame Maker

    Sold paints and things to do with art and did picture framing

"He was a gold beater by trade and was there for many years, until quite recently (1983). The gold beater's sign, arm and mallet, hung outside for many years. He supplied painting and drawing materials to schools as well."

- 188 Charles Loney, Cutler
- 186 Herbert Stephens, Watchmaker.

    Later it was Fielders, which first opened as a watchmakers and jewellers.

"All our showcases were plate glass and ebony. It was my job to pack them. We had to do it within an eighth of an inch. You started at the top and went right down. You cleaned the silver cutlery every morning – or it stained. Fielders was quite well known in the city for cutlery. People used to say to me 'We've still got your fish knives and forks'. The other side was fancy goods. We used to do a lot of whist drives for Whale Island, so mother was always on the look out for something different. Father was a working jeweller. I have a photo of him outside the first shop in a long white apron to catch the bits if any watch parts dropped. I've seen him open the back of a watch, give it a knock and hand it back - to the customer's astonishment. He just saw a speck of dust in the parts."

Miss F.V. Fielder

"A good watch cost 7/6d and it was 10/- for a workman's watch."

Since 1965 D.J. Gilbert has been here trading as Stock Mart Plastics, although the business was here earlier. The shop specialises in

Formica, kitchen worktops etc.

182   Osborne Stores Ltd., Grocers
       Another popular grocers where the housewife could buy her
       household needs, like a clothes cleaner called OMO at 3d and 6d a
       packet. In the 1960s it became one of the earliest supermarkets,
       Victor Value.

180   Miss Phyllis Hayward, Ladies Hairdresser
       Miss May Wheeler, Draper

178   Harry Tilney, Fruiterer

176   John's, Costumier

Buckland Congregational Church, first build in 1822 where the Shaftesbury
       Cinema (Bingo Hall) is now. The new church was built on the
       corner of Queens Road in 1869 to seat 900, with yellow, red and
       orange brickwork and an elaborate corner clock tower and slate
       fleche.

"In the early 1920s the minister was a Welshman, the Rev Miles who
could speak Welsh fluently. During the First World War there was a
contingent of Welsh Fusiliers stationed at Hilsea Barracks and for their
benefit part of the sermon was given in Welsh. The church hall was given
over to the Portsmouth Technical School. Most of my social life was
connected to Buckland Church from the end of the Second World War until
1950-51. I went to church most Sundays to meet the other local children
and to show of my Sunday best clothes, which were only worn that day.
Children did not play in the streets on Sunday, which was taboo in my
family. I also joined the Girl Guides and became what they called second.
The troop was divided into four groups. all named after birds. Unfortunately
the group I was in was called the 'Blue Tits', so I had to endure a lot of leg
pulling. There was also a Brownie Group for young girls and a Boys
Brigade, connected to the church. One Sunday a month we had church
parade. We marched from the back of the church, along Queens Road, to
the front entrance. The Girl Guides carried their colours down one aisle
and the Boys Brigade down the other. On the evening of the Guides
meeting, if you had 2d you could buy sweet cocoa powder in a square of
grease proof paper. You could then lick your finger and dip it into this
lovely sweet powder. As sweets were still rationed then it was a real treat!
I also signed the temperance pledge at this church to never drink alcohol!
Those were the days."

Una Jarman

here is Queens Road has a interesting series of villas and terraces in similar styles and dates to those in central Southsea – with the difference that the road is straight, not curved like Thomas Ellis Owen's developments.

160b J.B. Ward & Sons, Bakers with William Henderson, Dentist above.

"When I was about five my mother took me up there with terrible toothache. I was scared and he drew the tooth, for which my mother had to pay him 1/6d – would be the same as £5 today (1983). That gives you an idea of what people suffered, because they couldn't afford it – whether it was toothache or toe ache. Terrible days they were."

"If you were in funds you went to Wards the bakers. They used to sell bags of stale cakes left from the day before. You used to hope you'd get plenty of cream ones in your bag. They were all made in the shop."

160 William Gorfett, Chemist. Now Tremletts
158 William Cheeseman, Provision Stores
156 Herbert Claxton, Newsagent

"Clacky was a well known character in the district and delivered newspapers on a carrier cycle in all weathers dressed in a straw boater, jacket, plus fours and running shoes. His son was a well known racing cyclist at North End Cycle Club and used to race at Alexandra Park."

"It didn't matter if you wanted a paper of yesterday or yesteryear, go to Mr Claxton and he would have it. He had thousands of newspapers out the back all wrapped up in bundles. It was gaslit and at the back of the shop he had the Police Gazette. They had graphic cartoons about murders and court cases. Since the pictures were shut on Sundays you had nothing to do and he used to do a good trade in comics and tuppenny books. We used to go in there as kids to have a quick look. We never had a penny – but we never came out without one – he'd give us one."

Since 1958 the shop has been a hairdressers, Michaels.

St Stephens Church

The mission hall opened in 1882 and was replaced by a permanent building in 1899 designed by Reginald Crawley. It seated 650 and was a chapel of ease to St Mary's.

"St Stephens was a homely sort of church which was always full on a Sunday. We used to look forward to the family Sunday service. It was destroyed on 10th January 1941. Over the altar was a wooden cross and although the church was burnt to the ground the crucifix survived intact. I don't know if it's a miracle, but it does make one think."

The church was never replaced. Meetings were transferred to the Mission Hall, which later became part of Hoopers. There is now a suite shop on the site of the church.

152   Alfred Burgess, Outfitter

"Here we could buy our winter double breasted overcoat for 30/- and a made to measure suit for 42/-. It was the expensive end of the trade. A shirt for 7/6d elsewhere was 10/- here."

150   George Cox, Estate Agent

"A house to let in 1934 in, say Twyford Avenue with six rooms cost 17/- a week, or in Green Lane with a garage 18/6d a week (92.5p). Telephone Road was a little dearer at 21/- a week – well, after all, it is in Southsea! People often moved several times – when times were good you got something a little better, then if money was short you might look for something cheaper for a bit."

From 1971 to date has been a Pet Shop, Kingston Pet Stores.

148-146   PIMCO, Grocers

"They sold mainly their own brands of foods, like jams at sixpence ha'penny a jar and eleven pence ha'penny a jar. Their butter was 9d a pound."

142-140   The Shaftesbury Cinema, Portsmouth Town Cinemas Ltd.

The Shaftesbury Hall was opened on 10th May 1910, built by Cook & Bamber to seat 2,000 people, and it cost £7,000 to £8,000. It was claimed to have a fireproof construction. Mr Cook was a musician and on the right hand side was an organ for accompanying silent films. The pipes were arranged either side of the screen and were elaborately decorated with chinese dragons. Its music organ augmented the pit orchestra, during the film. The huge dome was surmounted by a bronze statue of Mercury in flight. The front was colonnaded.

"It really was something out of the ordinary. Before all the other cinemas the interior of the Shaftesbury was one of the most beautiful and was just like a theatre – like the Kings and the Theatre Royal. All round the walls and up at the top there were pictures painted taken from well known pictures like Constables. You could see right up into the dome and it was all beautiful colours. Film was in its infancy and they never knew if it would revert back into being a theatre."

"It was all that could be desired. It cost 2d to go to the pictures and that for a comfortable tip up seat. I remember the crowds on Saturday night to see the 'Lost World' it was a serial. The crowd stretched from the cinema right round to where Queens Road joins St Stephens Road. In November 1934 the silver screen showed the unforgettable Gracie Fields in 'Sing as we go'; a song which gave a much welcomed uplift in those hard times. Many a delivery boy could be heard whistling this tune. On one occasion, after a serious mining disaster, a vocalist sang for a week and a collection was taken in aid of the

The Shaftesbury

widows from the disaster, for in those days with no widows pensions or Social Security it was the orphanage or the workhouse. The song she sang was most applicable to the event, based on a dream a miner's daughter had dreamt: 'Don't go down the mine, Dad'."

"In the blitz the men who worked at Airspeed had gone there and there was a noisy film. A sign flashed onto the screen that an air raid was in progress: 'Persons wishing to leave may do so, or move to the back of the circle' when a bomb came through where the ceiling joins the wall. It was an incendiary and landed on the top of the capital ledge. It rested their but some men went out and collared a ladder. They found the shop next door – Woolworths – was completely burnt out, but they thought there was no danger and hardly anybody in the audience moved. The AFS got up and doused the incendiary for years afterwards you could see the temporary patch in the ceiling. I remember Nevil Shute (N.S. Norway, then director of Airspeed where I worked) walking around on Sunday night with his wife outside the cinema, looking at the stills, and if it was a good film he used to go in. He usually wore a grey suit and a grey trilby hat. I remember him about 1937/8 standing outside the Shaftsbury Cinema several times. Once the film was Moira Shearer in 'Private Lives'. Suddenly he and his wife went in. He used to have seats fairly close to the screen because of his vision. He also went to the Classic where later 'A Town Like Alice' was shown, which was based on the experience of Ridley Thompson in the jungle. At that time he was a very famous aircraft designer. He and Hessel Tittman developed the Airspeed Courier, the Airspeed Envoy, and were involved in the design of the R100 Airship. He used that experience in 'Slide Rule' about an aircraft mechanic."

Len Bufton

"Back in 1974 I was employed as a slater and tiler with Portsmouth City Council. One of my many tasks was to deal with emergencies. One such occurred on an afternoon in September 1974. Gale force winds were blowing all day, and much damage was done. I received a message to go to the Bingo Hall where the Statue of Mercury was swaying dangerously in the wind. Being atop a dome, access was very difficult, so the fire brigade were called. When Mercury finally reached the ground, it was realised that the statue was over seven feet tall. It also bore the dents made by an air rifle."

John Barker

"Quite recently someone took pot shots at Mercury, the green statue on the top standing on one leg on the dome of the Shaftsbury. They took him down and found he was peppered with shotgun pellets. Unfortunately trade was bad they had to close it down in 1959 when it became the Mecca Bingo. Four or five years ago they put up another floor across, there's a new cinema up above but that's closed now (1983)."

Since then it has changed hands and is now part of the Arnett Leisure Organisation.

138-136   F.W. Woolworth & Co.Ltd., Stores

"I was courting my young lady and I used to go up there every night at 7pm and she used to come out at 8.30 sometimes. They were supposed to close at 7pm on Saturdays it used to be 10pm. They used to keep open to 9pm before that and didn't close half past ten to eleven - all for ten shillings a week."

"Formerly it was the site of the Salvation Army Citadel which transferred in the 1920s to land formerly occupied by Mr Rowe the blacksmith at Powerscourt Road. Woolworths was destroyed by fire in the January 1941 blitz. After the war it became Tatfords, wholesale chemists supplying drugs to the chemists all over the city. The vans caused a nuisance in St Stephens Road, so they were moved to Burrfields as a non-conforming user about a year or to ago (in 1983). Now it's Edward's Leisure Centre; gambling machines, prize bingo and snooker."

134   PIMCO, Pastrycooks
      Bright orange brick edging around the windows with curious egg shaped panels. Later R.C. Dodson.
132   Darts, Printer
130   Swift & Presswell, Dyers & Cleaners
128   Herbert Cansdale, Pork Butcher
126   Charles Bowers, Tobacconist
124   Mrs Catherine Berry, Milliner
      Since 1977 Christopher, the shoe shop has had a branch here. They were founded in 1910 at Cosham.
122   Miss Lilian McDermott, Costumier
122   J. Fookes, Haulage Contractor
120   L.B.E. Gates, Wallpaper Merchant

"Nowadays there are hundreds and hundreds of wallpapers in the shops, but then most people would just have used distemper. It was only those with a little bit more money who had wallpapers. What there was didn't have much pattern on it – it was more mottled. It was about a shilling, and half a crown was the most you would pay for a roll. People used to whitewash their ceilings with lime. Back gardens were whitewashed too. Paper was often like anaglypta and was put on the bottom half of the wall and painted dark green or brown so as not to show the dirt. Later it was done cream. A lot of houses had a dado around to keep the back of chairs from marking the walls. Under the dado was lyncrusta and above was white. That's what skirting board are for, to keep your feet and furniture from damaging the plaster work. Some people used to paper a room right from the skirting to the ceiling with lining paper and then the painter would come in and marble it – say in the passage where it would give the effect of a marble hall – then it was varnished and it would last for years. When you got fed up with it you had a devil of a job getting it off. Wallpaper was often pasted up with flour and water. You had to be careful mixing it so you didn't get lumps. There was Lapp paste you could buy and Union Jack – it came in little cloth bags then, with a pull string at the top. Mind, nothing stuck as well as the old plain flour and water. I've heard that some people used mashed potato to thicken it up. Another thing was to stipple the walls – marbling was for the poshest room. You distempered in white or whatever and then made marks with a different colour, dipping bits of rag or sponge in an arc all over. Another idea before the War was to mark out panels with a plain filling and in the corners we had flowers painted. During the war when it was impossible to get paint and stuff I tried to touch it up once or twice with cream panels and bits of cream distemper with an old sponge. That style of decorating went right out and has never come back except for a few trendies."

118   Currys Ltd, Cycle Manufacturer.
       Still there in the 1980s selling televisions and washing machines. Now moved to Ocean Park, Burrfields. The shop is now a car parts centre.

"I bought my first bicycle at Currys for £3 18s when I was about 18. It cost me a shilling a week and it was a Raleigh. In 1927 I had a Hercules bike for £3 12s. There was Raleigh, Hercules, BSA, Enfield ... Nowadays there are so many French and Italian bikes about, and an ordinary bike is about £100. When you work it out it's no more compared to today's wages than it was then."

"When Pompey played at home all the houses along Frogmore Road and so on used to open up and for 2d or 3d you could take your bike through the house into the garden and they looked after it for you while the match was on. They all loved it when we were playing at home."

"All dockies went to work by bike – at outmuster you couldn't move for cyclists in Edinburgh Road. One night I came down that way at outmuster in a lorry and I wanted to turn into Charlotte Street. I waited and waited and there were no traffic lights in those days and they just wouldn't give way. So in the end I just put on my lights – main beams and all, and of course they were blinded and fell over, and those coming up behind went into the back of them. While they were sorting themselves out I went into Charlotte Street. Traffic lights weren't introduced until just before the war – the first ones in Pompey were in Elm Grove in 1934. Until then you just had police on point duty."

Frank Ford

116   Stephen Cummins, Fruiterer

"It had an ordinary house front and just a sash window. Mrs Cummins had a board outside on two boxes with the baskets of turnips and swede, so you had to lean right over these baskets to the window. Her son took over later and he had the front altered."

114   Miss Dorothy King, Watchmaker

An unusual occupation for a woman.

"Women go out to work today, but women have always worked for wages – they took in washing, or did dress making, or did outwork for the factories. The idea that women didn't work only applies to middle class women – not the bulk of women in the towns and country. In the two wars women came out and proved that they could do all the jobs like tram driving and so on. As time goes on things will get worse because there are no apprenticeships even for men – but then, there never have been for women.. They have always had a struggle to get trained to do trades and learn skills. The idea of education for women is still not accepted by everyone."

112   Mrs Emily Whitefield, Confectioner

110-104   Voller & Co., Corset and Underwear Makers

This was one of the original corset firms of which there used to be a large number, employing sailors' and soldiers' wives. It was rebuilt and extended to Binstead Road. The shop has no closed and the firm only trades by mail.

"It had frosted green windows and all the girls in there machining. Their entrance was in Binstead Road. It was only a factory with a little shop attached. Now it's a large glass fronted, flat roofed, two storey facade decorated with projecting grey bricks in panels."

"A ladies shop, but even a young boy can learn about female unmentionables, by studying the window display, and what a display! Ladies combinations, which stretched from neck to knee at 1/6d in a variety of colours – so we were not the sole wearer of this garment. Ladies' knickers, better known as bloomers at 1/- a pair. I have heard them known as 'passion killers'! An even stranger sight to boys eyes were the corsets of which I shall say no more except to state that they were priced at 12/11d. Ladies' stockings were 1/6d"

"There were two other corset factories further south towards Fratton: Leethams in St Marys Road, just closed as Twilfits (1983), and another off Church Road. They used to employ hundreds of women. In those days there was a lot of corset making in Portsmouth – girls and married women who worked to augment their poor income. I used to see them dashing home to lunch, not riding on the trams but walking because they couldn't afford the tram – even a 1d fare to North End. They wore long skirts in those days and heavy shoes. Some of the older women wore lace-up boots in winter, and they had hats – Tam O'Shanters. In those days it was five and a half day week, starting at 8 and knocking off at 5. There were lots of women working round there – for example at Palmer's Brush factory and in shops. They were hard days and the work was hard."

102   Campions (Bakers) Ltd.

here is Binsteed Road

"Binsteed Road school was down there. The road was named after Mr Binsteed, a solicitor who may have owned land in this part of Buckland. He was also on the Portsmouth School Board in the 1870s and 80s. The school was built in 1883 and celebrated its centenary this spring (1983) by inviting old pupils to a huge party. It's due to close soon because there are so few children of primary age."

Part of the school has been demolished and housing built on the site, the remainder is a community centre.

"I taught there in the 1960s when there were large classes. I did like the good flooring, heating, ventilation in the old fashioned schools. You could pull open the big windows to let the hot air rise. It was a good area to teach – a good working class area where the parents would take an interest in their children and also ask advice. They were very good and would help every time, like on open evenings. In the inner city areas with the Dockyard mateys' children, they were the salt of the earth: hardworking, supporting the school and looking after their children well. Different parts of the city have their own identity – more so than any other city – and each district is so proud: 'I'm Stamshaw – you're North End.' People are district."

100   Sidney Primmer, Baby Carriage Maker
       If you had a pram from Primmers you were doing yourself and
       your baby very well. It was the Eldorado of prams."
98   Thomas Hawes, Butcher
96   B. Duke, Ticket Writer
96   Ernest Payne, Optician

41

94   Miss Gertrude Palmer, Wool Merchant

"I remember when the lady in this shop was ill they spread peat two or three inches deep from Binsteed Road to Toronto Road to stop the noise of the traffic."

92   John Bryson, Florist

90   Miss Marion Albion, Stationer

88   Baker & Co., Pawnbroker

"The working class in those days were put upon. The people round Buckland were hard working but they were poor. No working person had any money. Whatever you earned had to be spent on food and it seemed the poorer you were the more there were in the family. Early in the morning you would see people lined up waiting to go into the pledge office. Anything pawnable was pawned. You'd even see men taking their tools in there. Work was very short and for a carpenter or joiner to get a job lasted 6 or 8 weeks – well you were alright then. Times were hard in them days."

"It's a Glass and Mirror Centre now – better than the things we used to see in the old pawnshop. It has a pretty slate roof with dormer windows and rusticated first floor windows."

here is Toronto Road

86   F.J. Mead, Provisions, Wines & Spirits.

"They called him the Salmon man – the shop had lots of tins of red salmon at 1/2d, sugar was sold in blue bags made into a cone and tucked in at the top. The delivery boy came with a three wheeled bike to deliver orders."

"I left Drayton Road School at Easter in 1934 and started work for Mr F.J. Mead. I worked from 8am until 7pm for three days a week, 8am 'til 1 on a Wednesday, 8am 'til 8pm on Friday and 8am 'til 9pm on Saturday. We had an off licence as well as groceries. Mr Voller of the corset firm had a regular order for two dozen small Guinness sent to his home in Kirby Road. Lyles Golden Syrup was 4s for a 1lb tin and 7½d for a 2lb tin. Sugar was 1¾d a pound, loose custard and cocoa 6d a pound, loose tea 4d to 6d a quarter, Betts biscuits were 6d a pound and they were good too! My wage for the first year was five shillings a week, with a promise of a 2/6 rise in the second year. I was told trade was bad so I got 6d. A couple if weeks later I got the hump for skylarking with the errand boy."

84   Alex Matthews, Draper

82   John Anderton, Tobacconist

"Displays of boxes of chocolates all tied up with ribbons."

78   George Cooper, Pork Butchers.

"They had a slaughter house up the back and drove the pigs up the alleyway at the side. His speciality was corn leg at 6d a quarter. We only had it when there was any extra money about. I can see him now in his starched apron and his thin rapier like knife. He could cut as well as any machine. And his faggots! All his stuff was made on the premises. The slaughterer was Mr Wakeford."

76   Sanders Bros (Stores) Ltd., Grocers.
       A tall three story house with an old peg tiled roof and Fareham Pots.

72A   The former entrance to New Road School, designed by Thomas Hellyer of Ryde as one of the first board schools in 1872. He added this entrance a few years later. The top of the pointed gothic arch is just visible over the doorway to the stone flagged passage. One of the school bells was above the passage, woe betide you if you got there after it stopped ringing. The school itself is at the back of the shops, occupying two facades designed by Thomas Hellyer, one pointed gothic arch with a linking string course and one flatter and curved.

74-72 W. Pink & Sons Ltd., Grocers
"A well known grocer with a chain of shops around the city. The main shop was in Commercial Road, and they had good quality provisions: for example Pink's self-raising floor 1½lbs for 3½d, currants 6d a pound, sultanas 8d a pound, raisins 6d a pound, a bar of Lifebuoy 3d, Stork Margarine 8d a pound, Campbells Condensed Tomato Soup 6d a tin. There is now more variety of food available. A lot of their wares were in wicker baskets on the floor – the dogs used to take advantage of this!"

70   Liptons Ltd., Provisions
"A rival firm with several branches all with the same layout."

68-66 Perkins Bros Ltd., Clothiers
"It sold working men's clobber."
"It was like two shops in one – one side dealt with outer garments, coats and suits and so on: the other side was for shirts and childrens' wear. Perched up in one corner behind parcels and boxes was a little office. When you bought something he put your money and bill in a cylinder on a wire on the ceiling and sent it round the shop to the office, where it was checked and your bill and change were sent back."
"Later it became Rodman's Menswear – they designed their own shirts."

64   Miss M. Brisbane, Milliner. Earlier the shop was Papps the music shop. Later it became Bennetts Music shop and now is Robert's

Piano Shop.

"They sold pianos in a long narrow shop. The pianos were made in Commercial Road, next to Lillies' Woodyard. If you paid £40 to £50 for one of these you had a good piano, not like the £1,000 you pay for an ordinary piano now."

62   Kingston Tavern, Thomas Pratt
>Listed from 1798 to 1885 as Buckland Brewery under various owners: David Orange (1798-1799), Charles Matthews (1880-1830), Fielding & Son (1832-1837), William Gough (1840-1865), John Holloway (1870-1885). Listed from 1886 to 1887 as the Brewery Tap then from 1888 to 1899 as a beer retailer. From 1902 listed as the Kingston Tavern.
>Pretty stained glass and enclosures around the name. Part of a three story terrace of eight shops.

"It was called the Shiny House. After the days work, to go to the local to meet a few friends and maybe enjoy a game of darts, made for a pleasant evening. A half pint of Brickwoods Sunshine Light Ale 4½d or maybe a dark ale 5½d. It slipped down very nicely."

60   Israel Press, Costumier

58   Mrs Mabel Hillman, Confectioner, now a Kebab house.

56   Maypole Dairy Co., Ltd

"Their sign was children dancing round the maypole and they dealt with diary products, with two foot cubes of butter and margarine. It brings back memories of buying butter – what a luxury – loose and watching the assistant pat it into shape with a pair of wooden pats – untouched by hand. Besides diary products, they sold their own brand tea which was popular at 2/- a pound."

54   Mrs A.K. Penny, Boot Stores. Now the Taj Mahal Indian Take-Away which was established in 1959.

"A queer little boot and shoe place."

52   J.B. Ward & Sons, Bakers. Above was Frank March, a solicitor and Ralph's detective agency.

"They had shops all over the town, and the bakery was at the top of New Road. They had a picture of a jolly baker in all their windows. The poorer families used to send the kids over with a pillowslip for the stale bread. They were the poor man's friend. Up at Alver Road they never brought anything but stale cakes and bread."

here is New Road

New Road was an important junction, not least for the trams.

"I used to stand for hours with the point boy to warn trams to stop or go over the single track sections. They had hand signals by day and by night used an oil lamp with red/green glass. Later high up on a lamppost a signal light was erected for use in daytime and at night. The colour was altered by a single switch on a small box on the post in reach of the point boy. On the electrification, 1901, of most tram points, point boys became redundant."

48   Charles Wilton, Drapers, later an electrical shop and now a Government Surplus shop. Above was a dentist, Ernest Middleton

46   Reginald Hoar, Butcher

44   William Hartley, Clothier

"They sold working mens' clothes – cloth caps, Melton trousers, Union and Oxford shirts (collarless) 4/11d for a good shirt and bib and brace overalls 4/11d. For casual wear you could have a very nice pair of grey flannel trousers commonly known as Oxford Bags for 7/6d. A tie 1/-: if you went to 1/6d you were going grand. You must remember this was a poor district. Men wore long pants and vests and Mr Hartley specialised in that sort of stuff, woollen vest, and socks and Trilby hats."

42   Wyndham, Milliner with a cranked shop front.

"In those days women always wore hats they weren't allowed in church without one. Hat shops in those days did more trade than they do now."

40   William Lock, Fruiterer

"They sold good fruit and Australian apples which stood on the side on the pavement on barrels – 3d a pound."

38   J.H. Dewhurst Ltd., Butchers. A white, pale blue and green ceramic panel remains of those days.

"A most popular buy would be a joint of beef for Sunday dinner. This would last for most of the week, in one way or another, but if it didn't last a calves head could be bought for a shilling or perhaps some rump steak at 10½d a pound"

36   George Bruton, Tobacconist

"Pipe tobacco could be bought loose, some smokers used to mix different brands such as half and ounce of coarse cut with half an ounce of something a little stronger. Winner Shag was popular at 8d an ounce. Cigarettes brands were Ardath, Craven Plain. Prices of cigarettes were around 10 for 6d"

34-32 Frederick Owens, Provision Merchant.

The poultry and pork butchers, the family working in the shop. Now a house again with a new domestic front.

"They sold game birds, fresh and dry fish on two big marble slabs. Next door they sold pork and cold pressed meats. They were a renowned good firm."

30   Emanuel Rosenblatt, Draper

Next were the gates to Campions Bakery later Portsmouth & Gosport Builders Guild, housing has now been erected on the site.

28-26 Midland Bank Ltd. A grand five bay building in Portland stone with a pillared entrance. When it closed it was used as office for a time before being converted into flats.

24-22 Campions (Bakers) Ltd

"They were a very big firm and really something as regards cakeshops. Their horses and carts used to deliver bread to people's houses all over the town. It was a beautiful shop, and all the girls wore black silk dresses and white fancy aprons and white cuffs and collars, a bit like Lyons 'Nippy Girls'. Later it was maroon coloured overalls with cream coloured cuffs and collars. In the centre window they had a display of wedding cakes and all the trophies they'd won."

"On offer were cracker cakes at 6d each, or perhaps you'd be tempted with a raspberry cream slice at 1d, 3d or 6d. Behind this shop was a large factory producing these lovely cakes and many more. I worked in this factory pre-war as a carpenters apprentice, helping to construct a sound-proof telephone and control office, and other fittings. One winter in the snow I was involved in constructing a long bicycle shed in their yard. We had a fire going and my mate and I took turns to have a warm by it. The girls in the factory were good to us, bringing out hot jugs of cocoa and cakes – very much appreciated. As another way to keep out the cold, brown paper was put in my boots and under my shirt."

22   Behind is a very fine peg tile roof, possibly eighteenth century with old sash windows.

20-18 George Corbin, Bootshop

"Most of their custom was 1/- a week. As a young man I never went anywhere else to buy shoes Spire brand I used to buy at 14/- a time - they were better class. Outside they had all boots and shoes on hooks fixed to battens, all prices."

16   The Old George, Mrs Alice Tobin

Listed from 1823 to 1981 as the Old George it was later a Bransbury's brewery house.

At the back is a variety of old slated roofs and Fareham pots. The frontage to Kingston Road is particularly handsome, two tone brown glazed design to the ground floor with yellow sunflowers in panels. It was converted into an old peoples day centre.

here is Little George Street

14-12 Lloyds Bank Ltd

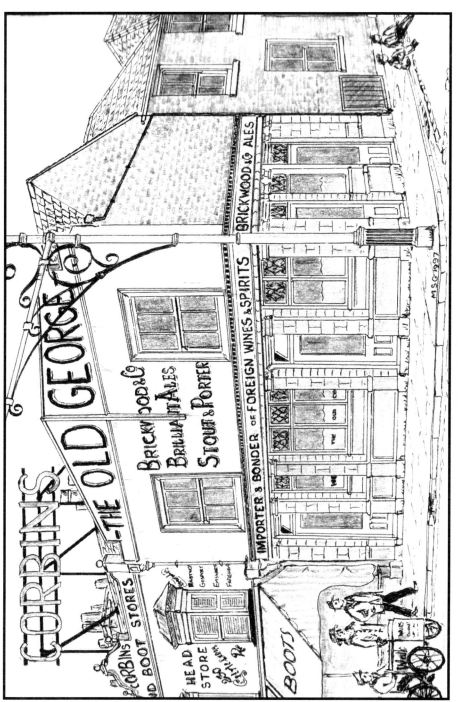

The Old George

A classical style facade with LLB medallion enclosed in curly leaves over the corner door. The building has since been converted into a Tridentine Mass Roman Catholic Church.

10   Model Shop, three storey with plain sash windows with an older roof.

8   Home & Colonial Stores Ltd.
        All standard design.

6   William Hunt, Brewer, Wines & Spirits

"They used to sell Hunts Tarragona in an oval bottle at about 4/- a quart bottle. We thought it was wonderful to have a bottle of this in the house at Christmas time. In the doorway the Pointsman used to shelter, sitting on an old crate. He had two long pointed sticks, one to clear out the muck and snow, and one to change over the points. On the corner of Lake Road trams went round towards Commercial Road one way and out to South Parade Pier the other way. The pointsman did it in shifts and they were both crippled. One was paralysed all down the side after being crushed against a wall by a tram, the other had a job to walk. Their only shelter was the shop doorway."

4-2   Timothy Whites Ltd., Chemists

"They were always the same pattern: on the left hand side near the door was always the chemist's department, and they always had a lantern light in the ceiling. At the back was a high three tiered counter with all the wares on shelves – you'd have a job to reach up to pay the man behind it, it was so high. You could buy all sorts of things in Timothy Whites and it was all loose. If you were decorating you'd go down there for two penn'eth of Linseed Oil."

"In 1934 Timothy Whites were selling gas filled light bulbs at 10½d or Crompton lamps were 1/6d. A very efficient copper bowl electric fire could be had for 5/-, or if you preferred an oil heater – a Valor would set you back 13/6d. To warm one's bed an aluminium hot water bottle cost 1/-. Meat safes with perforated zinc sides were also a popular buy (the counter part of the modern day fridge.) A special cone shaped kettle could be obtained for 2/3d. It had a reputation of boiling water fast."

Frank Ford

Later it was Gillains, a red, yellow and black striped facade, selling furniture and Nelson's Motorcycle Shop with upper storey white glazed with ballisters and ball finials. Both now gone, although Gillains still trades in Fratton Road.

"This corner with Lake Road was a very busy junction what with all the trams and Dockyardsmen. Remember, there were 10,000 men in the Dockyard in those days. There were bikes, horses and carts, trams and one or two motor cars. It warranted a traffic policeman. His name was Mr Young. He was a nice old chap. I don't know if he had any cases in his book. His thoughts were more to give you a clip round the ear. When he knocked off he'd have his cape under arm and a parcel with a few chops from the butcher or some vegetables out of the vegetable shop. All done in good faith and good feeling."

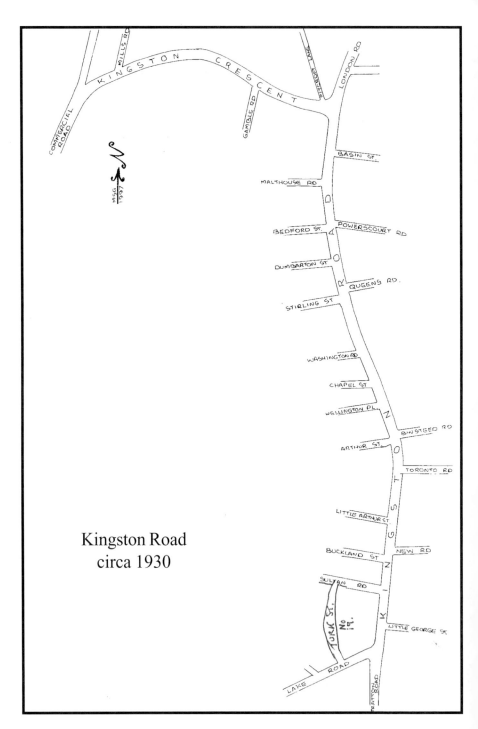

Kingston Road
circa 1930

NOTES

This booklet was compiled by the members of the W.E.A. Local History Group which meets at the New Road Adult Education Centre, Balliol Road, Buckland. The group is made up of local people who wish to record the history of ordinary peoples' lives and the streets in which they live. The group is very informal and welcomes new members who care to come to New Road on a Tuesday evening during term time or write to us.

Original Class Members:
> Mr A Albertolli, Len Bufton, Mrs Maud Dalley, Mrs Celia Clark, Frank Ford, Peter Galvin, Dave Jenkins, Frank Mullony, Stephen Pomeroy, Mrs Christine Richards, George Smith.

Current Class Members:
> Anton Cox, Frank Deacon, Betty Fowkes, Peter Galvin, Malcolm Garlick (Chairman), Ann Gilbert, Kevin Goldring, Pat Goldring, Len & Una Jarman, Stephen Pomeroy (Editor), Chris Redgrave, Frank & Jean Scott, Jeff Smith, Rita Wall, Margaret Webster (Treasurer)

Honorary Members:
> Olive Cook (Proofreader) Don Miles (Typesetting).

Affiliated Members:
> Des Beaumont, Morecambe, Lancashire.

Contributors:
> Mr John Barker, Mrs Kathleen Chard, Mr Jim Cramer, Miss F. Fielder, Mrs Joan Palmer (nee Errington), Mr S. Seward, Mr R. Shore, Mr O. Woon.

References:
> Portsmouth City Records Office, Portsmouth Central Library, Portsmouth Evening News, Portsmouth Papers.

This booklet is based on our earlier Kingston Road booklet. This has been revised and updated and we have also added Kingston Crescent.

WEA (Portsmouth Branch Local History Group)
Adult Education Centre
New Road Centre,
New Road, Buckland, Portsmouth
PO2 7QL

ISBN 1 873911 12 2

1873911122

Typeset & Printed in England
by
Printcraft, 108 Marmion Road, Southsea, Hants PO5 2BB